PERVERTED LOVE:
SIGN OF THE END TIMES

PERVERTED LOVE: SIGN OF THE END TIMES

by
Barbara Hicks Seguin
Author of Life Ministries, Inc.

Christian Publishing Services, Inc.
Tulsa, Oklahoma

Perverted Love: Sign of the End Times
ISBN 0-88144-109-0
Copyright © 1987 by
Barbara D. Hicks Seguin
Author of Life Ministries, Inc.
P. O. Box 701860
Tulsa, Oklahoma 74170-1860
and P. O. Box 3137
Center Line, Michigan 48015

Published by Christian Publishing Services, Inc.
P. O. Box 55388
Tulsa, Oklahoma 74155

CONTENTS

For the perverse are an abomination — extremely disgusting and detestable — to the Lord; but His confidential communion and secret counsel are with the uncompromisingly righteous — those who are upright and in right standing with Him.

The curse of the Lord is in and on the house of the wicked, but He declares blessed — joyful and favored with blessings — the home of the just and consistently righteous.

Proverbs 3:32,33

1
LOVE IS . . .

The world's meaning of love and God's meaning are grossly different. If you were to ask the average person on the street what he thinks of when you mention *love*, he would more than likely refer to some aspect of sexual gratification.

In his *Expository Dictionary of Biblical Words*,[1] W. E. Vine gives the following fifteen descriptions of the word *love*.

1. A profound, tender, passionate affection *for a person of the opposite sex.*

2. A feeling of warm personal attachment or deep affection, as for a parent, child, or friend.

3. A sexual passion or desire, or its gratification.

4. A person toward whom love is felt, a beloved person or sweetheart.

5. A direct address as a form of endearment.

6. A love affair.

7. A personification of sexual affection as Eros or Cupid.

8. An affectionate concern for the well-being of others, such as neighbors.

9. A strong predilection or liking for anything.

10. An object of this liking.

11. The benevolent affection of God for His creatures, or the reverent affection due from them to God.

12. Being in love, feeling deep affection or passion for a person, work, and so forth.

13. To make love: a) to woo; b) to embrace and kiss as lovers; c) to engage in sexual intercourse.

14. To have a profound tender passionate affection *for the opposite sex.*

15. To make love, to have intercourse with.

These descriptions allow room for all types of love, from the genuine to the counterfeit . . . from *agape* (real Christian love) to *phileo* (more of a tender affection) to *eros* (primarily sexual love, whether in or out of the marriage relationship).

Seducing spirits are on the rampage today, and these spirits are no respecters of persons. They have caused many a person to fall for perverse sexual release outside of the confines of the marriage union — from leaders in ministry to sinners on the street, from the respectable to the down and out.

The Holy Spirit through the apostle Paul gives very clear instructions about possessing (controlling) our bodies in Romans.

> I appeal to you therefore, brethren, and beg of you in view of [all] the mercies of God, *to make a decisive dedication of your bodies — presenting all your members and faculties — as a living sacrifice, holy (devoted, consecrated) and well pleasing to God,* which is your reasonable (rational, intelligent) service and spiritual worship.
>
> Do not be conformed to this world — this age, fashioned after and adapted to its external, superficial customs. But be transformed (changed) by the [entire] renewal of your mind — by its new ideals and its new attitude — so that you may prove [for yourselves] what is the good and acceptable and perfect will of God, even the thing which is good and acceptable and perfect [in His sight for you].
>
> **Romans 12:1,2**

Just as the mind must be renewed to believe and speak the Word of God, likewise the body must be brought into subjection to the Word.

Each person is responsible for dedicating himself completely to the Lord — spirit, soul, and *body.* Someone else cannot do it for you. You are to possess (or control) your own vessel.

Throughout this book, I have attempted to identify and encourage true *agape* (the God-kind) of love, both by defining what it is and what it is not.

[1] W. E. Vine, *Expository Dictionary of Old and New Testament Words* (OLd Tappan, New Jersey: Fleming H. Revell Company, 1981), Vol. 3, pp. 20-22.

2
GENUINE LOVE . . . *AGAPE*

By handling *real* or *genuine* money, a bank teller is able to detect the counterfeit. In the same manner, as we discover what *real* or *genuine* love is, we will be able to detect the counterfeit. We will be able to identify what genuine (or *agape*) love is and what it is not.

Agape, defined as "the God-kind of love," is the quality of love believers are to possess one toward another, both in the marriage union and in other relationships.

In his Greek study notes, A. S. Worrell says of the God-kind of love:

> . . . (It is) patient under trials; (it is) kind to every one, gentle, benevolent; (it is) not disturbed at the prosperity of others; (it) does not parade her own excellence; (it is not) inflated with high notions of herself; she is not only not grasping for more but she does not hold with a tight grip that which is really hers; (it is) never irritate or thrown off her balance; makes no note of evil done to her; she takes no part in anything wrong; truth and love are inseparable companions; (it) bears all trials of every kind; (it) believes all God's words and promises and never doubts His providence . . . While the gifts of the Spirit may become unnecessary and so pass away, love will never fail or cease to be.[2]

We find some of the characteristics of agape in the apostle Paul's first letter to the Corinthian church.

Love endures long and is patient and kind; love never is envious nor boils over with jealousy; it is not boastful or vainglorious, does not display itself haughtily.

11

It is not conceited — arrogant and inflated with pride; it is not rude (unmannerly), and does not act unbecomingly. Love [God's love in us] does not insist on its own rights or its own way, for it is not self-seeking; it is not touchy or fretful or resentful; it takes no account of the evil done to it — pays no attention to a suffered wrong.

It does not rejoice at injustice and unrighteousness, but rejoices when right and truth prevail.

Love bears up under anything and everything that comes, is ever ready to believe the best of every person, its hopes are fadeless under all circumstances and it endures everything [without weakening].

Love never fails — never fades out or becomes obsolete or comes to an end . . . .

1 Corinthians 13:4-8

W. E. Vine says of Christian (*agape*) love[3]:

. . . It has God for its primary object and expresses itself first of all in implicit obedience to His commandments . . . love seeks the welfare of others and works no ill to any . . . love seeks opportunity to do good to all men, and especially toward them who are of the household of faith.

It is quite obvious that selfishness has no place in *agape* love. Behind selfishness is pride and vanity. Pride is a conceited sense of one's superiority, and it is from the devil and his world. First John 2:16 says:

For all that is in the world, the lust of the flesh [craving for sensual gratification], and the lust of the eyes [greedy longings of the mind] and the pride of life [assurance in one's own resources or in the stability of earthly things] — these do not come from the Father but are from the world [itself].

As Christians, if we want to walk and live in the realm of *agape* love, we must take dominion over pride and allow it to have no place in our lives.

Remember, genuine or *agape* love accepts and loves the person but hates the sin. *Agape* love judges all situations by:

What would love do? The apostle Paul also talked about this kind of love to the Galatian assembly.

> **Brethren, if any person is overtaken in misconduct or sin of any sort, you who are spiritual — who are responsive to and controlled by the Spirit — *should set him right and restore and reinstate him,* without any sense of superiority and with all gentleness, keeping an attentive eye on yourself, lest you should be tempted also.**
>
> ***Bear (endure, carry) one another's burdens and troublesome moral faults,* and in this way fulfill and observe perfectly the law of Christ, the Messiah, and complete what is lacking [in your obedience to it].**
>
> **For if any person thinks himself to be somebody [too important to condescend to shoulder another's load], when he is nobody [of superiority except in his own estimation], he deceives and deludes and cheats himself.**
>
> **But let every person carefully scrutinize and examine and test his own conduct and his own work. He can then have the personal satisfaction and joy of doing something commendable [in itself alone] without [resorting to] boastful comparison with his neighbor.**
>
> **For every person will have to bear [be equal to under-standing and calmly receive] his own (little) load [of oppressive faults].**
>
> **Galatians 6:1-5**

As Christians, we are to help restore those who step out of *agape* into sin. In His love, we are to help them step back into God's grace so their blessing spout will not be clogged.

> **I give you a new commandment, that you should love one another: just as I have loved you, so you too should love one another.**
>
> **John 13:34**

---

[2] A. S. Worrell, *The Worrell New Testament,* p. 248.
[3] Vine, *Ibid,* p. 20.

3

AGAPE IS NOT THE LOVE OF MONEY

> For the love of money is a root of all evils; it is through this craving that some have been led astray, and have wandered from the faith and pierced themselves through with many acute [mental] pangs.

1 Timothy 6:10

A person who is not solidly anchored into the love of God may find that he has a problem of greed in his heart toward more money.

Sometimes, the more money people get, the more they think they need. Covetousness of money then takes root in their hearts. Believers are to covet only one thing — God Himself! Covetousness is an insatiable desire for worldly gain. In God's perspective, it is idolatry.

The Holy Spirit said through the apostle Paul:

> So kill (deaden, deprive of power) the evil desire lurking in your members — those animal impulses and all that is earthly in you that is employed in sin: sexual vice, impurity, sensual appetites, unholy desires, and all greed and covetousness, for that is idolatry [the deifying of self and other created things instead of God].

Colossians 3:5

Covetousness will exclude you from the Kingdom of God.

> For be sure of this, that no person practicing sexual vice or impurity in thought or in life, or one who is covetous — that is, who has lustful desire for the property of others and is greedy for gain — [for] that [in effect] is an idolater, has any inheritance in the kingdom of Christ and of God.

Ephesians 5:5

God is not talking about money that is being used for godly purposes, nor is He referring to possessing an abundance of money when the "love of money" has no stronghold in you.

There is nothing wrong with being a millionaire *if* it does not take precedence in your life. That is, your priorities should be in order — God first; your mate second; your family, third; and last of all, your ministry or career.

The use of money for buying property, the necessities of life, paying taxes and tithes, and the use of money for the Lord's work is not evil.

If all Christians were poor, all the churches in the world would have no alternative but to close. Money is a necessary ingredient for doing God's work. And certainly it is no testimony to God's promises nor to His goodness to drive down the road in a car that is blowing thick oil smoke out of the tail pipe, with a bumper sticker affixed which reads, "I believe in the God of prosperity" or "God meets all my needs."

Many of the godly patriarchs of old were very wealthy people. They had servants to meet their every need. Even the role model of a blessed and successful woman depicted in Proverbs 31 rose early each morning to assign tasks to her maids.

> **She rises while yet it is night and gets spiritual food for her household and assigns her maids her tasks.**
>
> **Proverbs 31:15**

Are you beginning to get the picture? God is not against wealth *as such*. In fact, wealth is part of God's blessings — but worrying or fretting about it and hoarding it is not!

The key to balance in the use of money is so simple: We are to love God first and our neighbors second. However, if money is our first love, then we are killing God's blessings before we even have them in hand.

4

LOVE IS NOT THE PRAISE OF MEN

And yet [in spite of all this] many even of the leading men — of the authorities and the nobles — believed and trusted in Him. But because of the Pharisees they did not confess it, for fear [that if they should acknowledge Him] they would be expelled from the synagogue.

For they loved the approval and the praise and the glory that come from men [instead of and] more than the glory that comes from God. — They valued their credit with men more than their credit with God.

But Jesus loudly declared, The one who believes on Me, does not [only] believe on and trust in and rely on Me, but [in believing on Me he believes] on Him Who sent Me.

And whoever sees Me sees Him Who sent Me.

John 12:42-45

Agape love does not seek the praise of men. A person motivated by the God-kind of love seeks God's approval.

Beware! Never love the praises of men, for they are fickle. Men can love you one moment and hate you the next. Also, the love of men will never let you tap into God's blessings. In fact, it will kill most of the blessings because you have your eyes on man instead of on God.

Some men have a motive behind their praises. They figure the more they stroke you with honey, the more you will do for them. On the other hand, there are some precious people who will praise you with a pure heart motive, wanting nothing in return.

The best and highest praises you can receive are from God. When you have His approval, His abundant blessings will overtake you.

Learn to be a God-praiser instead of a man-praiser. When you praise the Lord in song and in prayer, you literally open the windows of Heaven, because you are indicating that He is the only one worthy to be praised.

5
LOVE IS NOT LUST

Lust is evil desire and self-deception. Satan is the author of lust, the counterfeit of love.

[But] he who commits sin (who practices evil doing) is of the devil — takes his character from the evil one; for the devil has sinned (has violated the divine law) from the beginning. The reason the son of God was made manifest (visible) was to undo (destroy, loosen and dissolve) the works the devil [has done].

No one born (begotten) of God [deliberately and knowingly] habitually practices sin, for God's nature abides in him — His principle of life, the divine sperm, remains permanently within him — and he cannot practice sinning because he is born (begotten) of God.

By this it is made clear who take their nature from God and are His children, and who take their nature from the devil and are his children: no one who does not practice righteousness — who does not conform to God's will in purpose, thought and action — is of God; neither is anyone who does not love his brother [his fellow believer in Christ].

Because this is the message — the announcement — which you have heard from the first, that we should love one another.

[And] not be like Cain who [took his nature and got his motivation] from the evil one and slew his brother. And why did he slay him? Because his deeds (activities, works) were wicked and malicious and his brother's were righteous — virtuous.

1 John 3:8-12

Random House Dictionary describes *lust* as meaning "uncontrolled or illicit sexual desire or appetite; passionate or overmastering desire for power or sex."[4] It describes lust as one of the seven deadly sins:

19

"Passion, strong desire, craving, bodily appetite, fleshly desire, sexuality, libidinousness, lasciviousness, lewdness, salaciousness, satyriasis, nymphomania, carnality, lechery — desire intensely, crave, have a passion for, covet, hunger for; seek sexually, be lascivious, be libidinous, be lewd."[5]

A lustful person, whether he is pursuing sex or material possessions, has the "big me" at the center of his life.

Lust comes from an evil heart. An evil heart rarely is born overnight. The person usually begins evil acts on a small scale, such as telling lies or stealing, but he progressively moves into deeper realms of sin to the point that his conscience loses its sensitivity.

The art of evil doing or lusting for things becomes normal to him. I have found this to be true of many people who are in prisons today. They did not start with armed robbery. They began stealing small things — then moved into big time wrongdoing!

The Word of God says:

> But what comes out of the mouth comes from the heart, and this is what makes a man unclean and defiles [him].
>
> For out of the heart come evil thoughts (reasonings and disputings and designs) such as murder, adultery, sexual vice, theft, false witnessing, slander and irreverent speech.
>
> **Matthew 15:18,19**

The Bible says lust is deceitful.

> Strip yourselves of your former nature — put off and discard your old unrenewed self — which characterized your previous manner of life and becomes corrupt through lust and desires that spring from delusion.
>
> **Ephesians 4:22**

The Bible says lust is enticing.

> But every person is tempted when he is drawn away, enticed and baited *by his own evil desire (lust, passions).*
>
> Then the evil desire when it has conceived gives birth to sin, and sin when it is fully matured brings forth death.
>
> Do not be misled, my beloved brethren.
>
> **James 1:14-16**

1:14-16

Notice, James said that we are enticed by *our own evil desire*. We are misleading ourselves if we think lust is not a subtle device of the devil to kill our blessings. There is no way to receive the creative thoughts of the Lord and His abundant blessings when your mind is lusting after someone or something.

Many people have been hurt by lust, particularly in a marriage relationship. The Bible says lust is hurtful.

> But those who crave to be rich fall into temptation and a snare, and into many foolish (useless, godless) and hurtful desires that plunge men into ruin and destruction and miserable perishing.
>
> 1 Timothy 6:9

While the husband sits by his wife's side, his eyes roam the room to give a flirtatious look to another woman. Now, of course, the husband is not always the problem. In many cases, it is the wife who is the flirt. An affair never starts in the bed. It starts with a little eye contact, a cute smile, and a honey tongue. Later comes the death of the family unit and the marriage. No one is immune to Satan's subtle tactics. Protect yourself. Flee the devil's devices the minute you discern a wrong atmosphere.

The Bible indicates that lust temptations are numerous.

> For among them are those who worm their way into homes and captivate silly and weak-natured and spiritually dwarfed women, loaded down with [the burden of their] sins, [and easily] swayed and led away by various evil desires and seductive impulses.
>
> 2 Timothy 3:6

At some point, God gives the unregenerate up to their own evil ways. An unregenerate person usually knows about the ways of God, yet chooses of his own free will to pursue the perverseness of his old nature.

> Therefore God gave them up in the lusts of their [own] hearts to sexual impurity, to the dishonoring of their bodies among themselves, abandoning them to the degrading power of sin.

Because they exchanged the truth of God for a lie and worshipped and served the creature rather than the Creator, Who is blessed forever! Amen — so be it.

For this reason God gave them over and abandoned them to vile affections and degrading passions. For their women exchanged their natural function for an unnatural and abnormal one;

And the men also turned from natural relations with women and were set ablaze (burned out, consumed) with lust for one another, men committing shameful acts with men and suffering in their own bodies and personalities the inevitable consequences and penalty of their wrong doing and going astray, which was [their] fitting retribution.

And so, since they did not see fit to acknowledge God or approve of Him or consider Him worth the knowing, God gave them over to a base and condemned mind to do the things not proper or decent but loathsome;

Until they were filled — permeated and saturated — with every kind of unrighteousness, iniquity, grasping and covetous greed, [and] malice. [They were] full of envy and jealousy, murder, strife, deceit and treachery, ill will and cruel ways. [They were] secret backbiters and gossipers,

Slanderers, hateful to and hating God, full of insolence, arrogance [and] boasting; inventors of new forms of evil, disobedient and undutiful to parents.

[They were] without understanding, conscienceless and faithless, heartless and loveless [and] merciless.

Though they are fully aware of God's righteous decree that those who do such things deserve to die, they not only do them themselves but approved and applaud others who practice them.

Romans 1:24-32

Glory to God! The Spirit of God has spoken. Such people walk after the flesh, living as if they will be on Earth forever. They are blinded, and their lives need to be rearranged by God.

Proverbs 7 gives a description of the subtleties of a prostitute as she allures men to her bedroom. Verse 27 states clearly that the destiny is Hell for those who choose to pursue the smooth words of the prostitute.

> Her house is the way to Sheol [Hades, the place of the dead] going down to the chambers of death.

Other verses in Proverbs 9 confirm Hell as the destiny for those entertained by the prostitute.

> Stolen waters [pleasures] are sweet [because they are forbidden], and bread eaten in secret is pleasant.

> But he knows not that the shades of the dead are there [specters haunting the scene of past transgressions], and that her invited guests are [already sunk] in the depths of Sheol [the lower world, Hades].

> Proverbs 9:17,18

Without any doubt, lust will kill your blessings. It will bring destruction to you — the temple of God. Lust takes you on a downward path, causing you to constantly crave for the forbidden. Lust is a selfish means of gratification with no regard for the other person involved or for the consequences. The conscience becomes seared, and we are to strive for a clear conscience.

> Therefore I always exercise and discipline myself — mortifying my body [deadening my carnal affections, bodily appetites and worldly desires], endeavoring in all respects — to have a clear (unshaken, blameless) conscience, void of offense toward God and toward men.

> Acts 24:16

Through the grace of God provided by the shed blood of Jesus His Son, we have been given a way of escape from lust (and all other forms of evil).

> By means of these He has bestowed on us His precious and exceedingly great promises, so that through them you may escape (by flight) from the moral decay (rottenness and corruption) that is in the world because of covetousness (lust

and greed), and become sharers (partakers) of the divine nature.

2 Peter 1:4

---

[4] *Random House Dictionary,* Revised Edition (New York: Random House, Inc.) Copyright © 1984.

[5] Ibid.

6
LOVE IS NOT HOMOSEXUALITY

Random House Dictionary defines *homosexuality* as "a sexual desire or behavior toward a person or persons of one's own sex."[6] *Homosexual* is a generic term, but usually today is used for men. However, this definition is applicable to the lifestyle of a lesbian (a female homosexual) as well.

The immortality of man's nature is implicit in the creation of man in God's image,[7] the Word reveals.

> So God created man in His own image, in the image and likeness of God He created him: male and female He created them.
>
> **Genesis 1:27**

God created us in His own image . . . male and female, He created us. The Bible does not say, "Male and male, He created them," nor does it say, "Female and female, He created them."

In the 1980s, we are beginning to see the devastating consequences of homosexuality. Is the immorality of man killing his blessings? Let us look to the Word of God and find the answers.

The type of affection exchanged in a homosexual or lesbian relationship is not love, but abuse and sexual perversion.

As we see from Scripture, homosexuality was a problem in Lot's day. God was not any more pleased with it thousands of years ago than He is today.

> And they called to Lot, and said, Where are the men who came to you tonight? Bring them out to us, that we may know [be intimate with] them.
>
> And Lot went out of the door to the men, and shut the door after him.

And said, I beg of you, my brothers, do not behave so wickedly.

Look now, I have two daughters who are virgins; let me, I beg of you, bring them out to you, and you do as you please with them; but only do nothing to these men, for they have come under the [protection] of my roof.

But they said, Stand back! And they said, This fellow came in to live here temporarily and now he presumes to be [our] judge! Now we will deal worse with you than with them. So they rushed at and pressed violently against Lot, and came close to breaking the door.

But the men [the angels] reached out and pulled Lot into the house to them, and shut the door after him.

And they struck the men that were at the door of the house with [dazzled] blindness, from the youths to the old men, so that they wearied themselves [groping] to find the door.

And the [two] men asked Lot, Have you any others here? Sons-in-law, or your sons, or daughters? Whomever you have in the city, bring them out of this place.

For we will spoil and destroy [Sodom], for the outcry and shriek against its people has grown great before the Lord; and He has sent us to destroy it.

Genesis 19:5-13

These men intended to have deviate sexual relations with "men" whom they did not know were God's angels. The hand of God brought judgment on the men of Sodom. They did not just lose their blessings; they lost their lives. The city where they had lived was destroyed as well.

The whole land is brimstone and salt, and a burned waste, not sown or bearing anything, where no grass can take root, like the overthrow of Sodom and Gomorrah with Admah and Zeboiim, which the Lord overthrew in His anger and wrath.

Deuteronomy 29:23

A footnote in *The Amplified Bible* says[8]:

"The Bible emphasizes the 'security of the saints,' but it is equally emphatic concerning the insecurity of those in conscious and continued indifference to God."

Paul wrote in Galatians 6:8:

> For he who sows to his own flesh (lower nature, sensuality) will from the flesh reap decay and ruin and destruction; but he who sows to the Spirit will from the Spirit reap life eternal.

The Word makes it very clear that those who participate in perverse sexual behavior are headed literally for a destiny in Hell.

> Do you not know that the unrighteousness and the wrongdoers will not inherit or have any share in the kingdom of God? Do not be deceived (misled); neither the impure and immoral, nor idolaters, nor adulterers, nor those who participate in homosexuality,

> . . . Will inherit or have any share in the kingdom of God.

> 1 Corinthians 6:9,10

The lower natures of men or women will destroy them if they do not take control of the flesh. In God's eyes and by His standards, there can never be acceptance of immoral living. It totally disqualifies man from receiving any of God's blessings.

True heart repentance is the key to restoration of God's blessings. However, with true heart repentance also comes a total turning away from the sins of man's old nature. Homosexual activities are totally repulsive to God. So are all other perverse sexual activities.

> You shall not lie with a man as with a woman; it is an abomination.

> Whoever commits any of these abominations shall be cut off from among [his] people.

> So keep My charge; do not practice any of these abominable customs which were practiced before you, and defile yourselves by them. I am the Lord your God.

> Leviticus 18:22,29,30

Homosexuality, lesbianism, and perverted sex of any kind open the door to God's fury.

Sexual vice makes the homosexual (or lesbian) a slave to his passions. He is totally out of control and daily sinks lower into Satan's pit of Hell by his own free will. We are commanded to abstain from sexual vice, for it will kill God's blessings in our lives.

> For this is the will of God, that you should be consecrated — separated and set apart for pure and holy living: that you should abstain and shrink from all sexual vice.
>
> 1 Thessalonians 4:3
>
> Beloved, I implore you as sojourners, strangers and exiles [in this world] to abstain from the sensual urges — the evil desires, the passions of the flesh [your lower nature] — that wage war against the soul.
>
> 1 Peter 2:11

It is not too difficult to see that the homosexual is accursed. He, by his own free choice, performs a forbidden act, creating impenetrable hardness in his heart. How any man or woman of God (any believer) can adapt to this kind of lifestyle is beyond my comprehension. Not only do people call such a person names behind his back, but there is no compassion from the natural world should that person become a victim of AIDS or some other disease.

Many in the natural world have no respect for this lifestyle, although they may give lip service to "gay" rights. F. Scott Fitzgerald — one of this century's "great" writers, according to the literary world, and a man who mixed with the literati and social elite, as well as with Hollywood and Broadway artistic types — looked on homosexuality as an aberrant form of sex. He wrote, "Fairies: Nature's attempt to get rid of soft boys by sterilizing them."[9]

Christians are not the only ones who consider people with this kind of sexual lifestyle perverted. The natural world pokes fun at them with various names such as "tulips," "fairies," "fruitcakes," and "gays" — a complete misnomer! Names for lesbians are even cruder.

In today's climate of moral anarchy, there has come to be more sympathy for homosexuals and lesbians among liberals and in the media. However, the "sympathy" is not compassion but a manifestation of the anti-authority and anti-Christian philosophy that is attempting to take hold of America. It is an everyone-has-the-right-to-do-his-own-thing attitude, a belief that, "There is no right or wrong. Each person's choice of lifestyle is as acceptable as any other's." This is even being taught in many public school textbooks today under the guise of sex education or sociology, and in colleges, as "situational ethics."

Thank God, most Christians do have compassion on those living in homosexuality, although they do not approve. We call this lifestyle *sin*, not just "a different choice in sexuality."

Sodom and Gomorrah were judged for their perverse sexual acts, and those practicing this lifestyle today also will be judged. In fact, in my opinion, I believe today's epidemic of AIDS is only a part of the judgment to come for homosexuals.

> **The face of the Lord is against those who do evil, to cut off the remembrance of them from the earth.**
>
> **Psalm 34:16**

---

[7] *Wycliffe Bible Encyclopedia* (Chicago: Moody Press, p. 1053, 1054) Copyright © 1975.

[8] *The Amplified Bible, Old Testament* (Grand Rapids: Zondervan Publishing House, p. 250) Copyright © 1962,1964.

[9] *The International Thesaurus of Quotations* (New York: Harper & Row, Publishers, p. 283) Copyright © 1970. F. Scott Fitzgerald, "The Notebooks," *The Crack Up* (1945).

7

SINNER: RECIPIENT OF GOD'S BLESSINGS?

My son, if sinners entice you, do not consent.

If they say, Come with us, let us lie in wait to shed blood, let us ambush the innocent without cause [and show that his piety is in vain];

Let us swallow them up alive as does Sheol [the place of the dead], and whole, as those who go down into the pit [of the dead];

We shall find and take all precious goods [when our victims are put out of the way], we shall fill our houses with plunder;

Throw in your lot among us [they insist], and be a sworn brother and comrade; let us all have one purse in common.

My son, do not walk in the way with them, restrain your foot from their path;

For their feet run to evil, and they make haste to shed blood.

For in vain is the net spread in the sight of any bird;

But [when these men set a trap for others] they are lying in wait for their own blood, they set an ambush for their own lives.

So are the ways of every one who is greedy of gain; such [greed for plunder] takes away the life of its possessors.

Proverbs 1:10-19

The sinner is not motivated by the God-kind of love. In fact, by his lack of knowledge, he kills God's blessings by the wrong choices he makes.

As believers in the Lord Jesus Christ, we are admonished to run *from* the path of the sinner.

For a sinner to receive the blessings that belong to him, he must repent and turn from a life of sin. There is forgiveness for sinners through the Lord Jesus Christ. Paul was a murderer. Peter failed in love and friendship, and Jesus forgave him.

> **And Peter answered them, Repent — change your views, and purpose to accept the will of God in your inner selves instead of rejecting it — and be baptized every one of you in the name of Jesus Christ for the forgiveness of and release from your sins; and you shall receive the gift of the Holy Spirit.**
>
> **Acts 2:38**

Peter preached a Gospel of forgiveness. He allowed Jesus to forgive him. This same attitude of humility must fill the heart of the sinner for him to turn from the dead-end road that he is on . . . a road that heads straight into Hell, with no opportunity to take a side trip.

The *Wycliffe Bible Encyclopedia* writes about the Parable of the Prodigal Son in this way[10]:

> Right now they are the prodigal sons whom Luke wrote about in his gospel. This parable of Christ's is considered the crown and pearl of all Christ's parables because of its lucid portrayal of gospel truth. Christ structured this parable around the Jewish custom of that time, whereas the father could assign his possessions to his heirs during his lifetime. He could hand over easily an allotment to the young son, and which he did. The elder son never asked for his share but stayed dutifully with his father. Soon the younger son was tired of sinning and out of all his money. He decided while feeding swine (which was the only work that he could find) that he would go back to his father and repent. He expected to be scorned and rejected and maybe put to work as a hired hand in a very demeaning position. But he was truly sorry and went home with a sincere heart of repentance.

However, instead of scorn, his father was joyful and enthusiastic at his return. Well, God's welcome to the repentant sinner is the same.

Jesus is saying to every sinner or backslidden person today, "Come back to Me. All is forgiven and forgotten." Your salvation is free through the grace of God.

As Christians we should, even in the pattern of our lifestyle, teach the blind sinner why he is killing God's true blessings of health, love, and prosperity. If the sinner will not turn from his wicked ways, we as Christians still *have no right to rejoice* when they fall victim to AIDS or some other disease.

Proverbs 24:17 and 18 says:

> Rejoice not when your enemy falls, and let not your heart be glad when he stumbles or is overthrown;
>
> Lest the Lord see it, and it be evil in His eyes and displease Him, and He turn away His wrath from him [to expend it upon you, the worse offender].

As believers, we are not called to *judge* those in perverse sexual activities. Yet, we need to realize that it is each person's individual choice to throw away the unregenerate lifestyle and thereby resurrect God's blessings in their lives.

There always are conditions to God's promises. His promises are for the willing and obedient . . . those who know the Lord's voice and who walk with Him every second of their waking hours.

> If you are willing and obedient, you shall eat the good of the land.
>
> Isaiah 1:19
>
> If you will listen diligently to the voice of the Lord your God, being watchful to do all His commandments which I command you this day, the Lord your God will set you high above all the nations of the earth,
>
> And all these blessings shall come upon you and overtake you, if you heed the voice of the Lord your God.
>
> Blessed shall you be in the city, and blessed shall you be in the field.

Blessed shall be the fruit of your body, and the fruit of your ground, and the fruit of your beasts, the increase of your cattle, and the young of your flock.

Blessed shall be your basket and your kneading trough.

Blessed shall you be when you come in, and blessed shall you be when you go out.

The Lord shall cause your enemies who rise up against you to be defeated before your face; they shall come out against you one way, and flee before you seven ways.

The Lord shall command the blessing upon you in your storehouse, and in all that you undertake; and He will bless you in the land which the Lord your God gives you.

The Lord will establish you as a people holy to Himself, as He has sworn to you, if you keep the commandments of the Lord your God, and walk in His ways.

And all people of the earth shall see that you are called by the name [and in the presence of] the Lord; and they shall be afraid of you.

And the Lord shall make you have a surplus of prosperity, through the fruit of your body, of your livestock, and of your ground, in the land which the Lord swore to your fathers to give you.

The Lord shall open to you His good treasury, the heavens to give the rain of your land in its season, and to bless all the work of your hand; and you shall lend to many nations, but you shall not borrow.

And the Lord shall make you the head, and not the tail; and you shall be above only, and you shall not be beneath, if you heed the commandments of the Lord your God, which I command you this day, and are watchful to do them.

And you shall not go aside from any of the words which I command you this day, to the right hand or to the left, to go after other gods to serve them.

Deuteronomy 28:1-14

---

[10] *Wycliffe Bible Encyclopedia*, p. 1405.

8
PERVERTED LOVE: SIGN OF THE END TIMES?

The heart motive behind perverted love is amusement. How tragic! The entertainment of such a person is lust of the eyes, lust of the flesh, and the pride of life — deadly sins. The problem behind this type of lifestyle is that the person does not believe there is a God and therefore does not rely on and trust in Him. God's Word says we shall not be disappointed if we rely on and trust in Him.

> . . . No man who believes in Him — who adheres to, relies on and trusts in Him — will [ever] be put to shame or disappointed.
>
> **Romans 10:11**

While immorality is amusement to the person who participates in it, God's Word warns against these perverse acts.

> But [instead it is you] yourselves who wrong and defraud, and that even your own brethren [by so treating them]!
>
> Do you not know that the unrighteous and the wrongdoers will not inherit or have any share in the kingdom of God? Do not be deceived (misled); neither the impure and immoral, nor idolaters, nor adulterers, nor those who participate in homosexuality.
>
> **1 Corinthians 6:8,9**

Homosexuals and lesbians are not physically dead; but they are spiritually dead, yet while they live. (1 Tim. 5:6.)

God's Word indicates that this perversion *will be prevalent in the last days*. Many men and women of God believe that we are in the last of the last days.

> But understand this, that in the last days there will be set in perilous times of great stress and trouble — hard to deal with and hard to bear.

> [They will be] treacherous (betrayers), rash [and] inflated with self-conceit. [They will be] lovers of sensual pleasures and vain amusements more than and rather than lovers of God.
>
> 2 Timothy 3:1,4

> And they did not know or understand until the flood came and swept them all away, so will be the coming of the Son of man. . . .
>
> Watch, therefore — give strict attention, be cautious and active — for you do not know in what kind of a day [whether a near or remote one] your Lord is coming.
>
> Matthew 24:39,42

A perverted lifestyle is not characteristic of a true Christian. However, as Christians, our role is walking with God in altruism (living for the good of others) and helping the weak who are aborting the true blessings of God.

> In everything I have pointed out to you [by example] that, by working diligently thus we ought to *assist the weak*, being mindful of the words of the Lord Jesus, how He Himself said, It is more blessed — makes one happier and more to be envied — to give than to receive.
>
> Acts 20:35

We are to assist the weak, but the questions we must ask ourselves are, "Are these people weak only in the flesh, or do they have a spirit of rebellion, a spirit of lust, and do they really want help to turn from their lifestyles of sin? Or do they want us to accept them as they are and thereby compromise our Christianity?"

Reader, you must make your own choice on how you will handle such a person when face to face. Are you going to try to save his soul? Jesus said to assist the weak. I think that means to love the person but hate the deed, while trying to bring about his salvation as time goes on.

Your guide should be, "What would *agape* love do?"

Who is causing this apostasy (falling away from God's truth)? Satan is the source of it all.

> **Simon, Simon (Peter), listen! Satan has asked excessively that (all of) you be given up to him — out of the power and keeping of God — that he might sift (all of) you like grain.**
>
> **Luke 22:31**

Satan loves sifting people as grain, but he particularly delights in sifting God's people. His subtleties also keep the homosexual or lesbian under the curse.

> **They have eyes full of harlotry, insatiable for sin. They beguile and bait and lure away unstable souls. Their hearts are trained in covetousness — lust, greed. [They are exposed to cursing,] children of a curse!**
>
> **Forsaking the straight road they have gone astray; they have followed the way of Balaam, [the son] of Beor, who loved the reward of wickedness.**
>
> **2 Peter 2:14,15**

Satan has a stronghold on the minds of homosexuals and lesbians. Wickedness starts in the mind before the act of immorality occurs.

Today, there is a lawlessness (anarchy) in our society that manifests itself in moral looseness. Moral instability is not always detectable by outward appearances, for the outward appearance many times conceals an inner rottenness of the heart.

I believe perverted love is without a doubt a gigantic sign of end times — a sign of the closeness of Jesus' return.

9

BLESSINGS FOR THE "APPLE OF HIS EYE"

A lifestyle of perverted love will bring continued curses, then death. On the other hand, walking in God's ways will bring protection. As saints (believers), we are the apple (or pupil) of God's eye.

You may be asking, "What is the apple of God's eye?"

This Biblical idiom signifies something of great value. The apple (literally a play on words meaning "little man") refers to the tiny image man sees of himself reflected in the pupil of another person's eye.

Moses talked about God's omniscience: . . . **He scanned him (penetratingly), He kept him as the pupil of His eye** (Deut. 32:10).

God forever sees all things done in secret or in the open. The sinner cannot imagine that God sees everything he does! On the other hand, the believer wants God's attention and care. He says, [Lord], **keep and guard me as the pupil of the eye; hide me in the shadow of Your wings** (Ps. 17:8).

The blinders have been removed from the Christian's eyes, while the sinner is yet in total darkness. As we obey Proverbs 7:2, we become eligible to receive God's best blessings: **Keep my commandments and live, and keep my law and teaching as the apple (the pupil) of your eye.**

> For thus said the Lord of hosts, after His glory had sent me [His messenger] to the nations who plundered you, for he who touches you touches the apple or pupil of His eye.
>
> **Zechariah 2:8**

As a child of God, not only are we protected, but we (and our households) are heirs of all God's promises. We are redeemed from all of the curses.

> To the end that through [their receiving] Christ Jesus, the
> blessing [promised] to Abraham might come upon the
> Gentiles, so that we through faith might [all] receive [the
> realization of] the promise of the (Holy) Spirit.

> Galatians 3:14

If you are right now living a perverted lifestyle, my
prayer is that you will receive the Word of God like apples
of gold to help you change.

> A word fitly spoken and in due season is like apples of
> gold in a setting of silver.

> Proverbs 25:11

> The path of the wise leads upward to life, that he may
> avoid the gloom in the depths of Sheol (Hades).

> Proverbs 15:24

Through the amazing grace of God, you can have a new
life full of God's blessings. Come and drink the living water
Jesus has supplied for eternal life.

> But whoever takes a drink of the water that I will give
> him shall never, no never, be thirsty any more. But the water
> that I will give him shall become a spring of water welling
> up (flowing, bubbling) continually with him unto (into, for)
> eternal life.

> John 4:14

As you turn from a life of sin and make Jesus Christ
the Lord of your life, He promises you a new nature.

> Therefore if any person is (ingrafted) in Christ, the
> Messiah, he is (a new creature altogether,) a new creation;
> the old (previous moral and spiritual condition) has passed
> away. Behold, the fresh and new has come!

> But all things are from God, Who through Jesus Christ
> reconciled us to Himself (received us into favor, brought us
> into harmony with Himself) and gave to us the ministry of
> reconciliation — that by word and deed we might aim to bring
> others into harmony with Him.

> 2 Corinthians 5:17,18

Therefore, as you are reconciled with God, you
automatically stop killing your inherited blessings when you

walk in the law of love by obedience. Jesus knows of your affliction and distress. He is holding out His hands to you right now saying, "Come to Me, and I will even change your name, dear one. I love you."

> He who is able to hear, let him listen to and heed what the Spirit says to the assemblies (the churches). To him who overcomes (who conquers) I will give to eat of the manna that is hidden, and I will give him a white stone, with *a new name* engraved on the stone which no one knows or understands except he who receives it.

> Revelation 2:17

The prophet Isaiah also said you would be called by a new name when you become a member of God's family.

> And the nations shall see your righteousness and vindication — your rightness and justice [not your own but His ascribed to you] — and all kings shall behold your salvation and glory and *you shall be called by a new name,* which the mouth of the Lord shall name.

> Isaiah 62:2

10
REVERSE THE CURSE

There are several things a person can do to reverse the curse if they have been living a perverted sex life.

1. Repent . . . run from your sin into the arms of God by accepting Jesus as your Lord and Savior.

> I tell you, No; but unless you repent — [that is,] change your mind for the better and heartily amend your ways with abhorrence of your past sins — you will all likewise perish and be lost [eternally].
>
> Luke 13:3

> He who covers his transgressions will not prosper, but whoever confesses and forsakes his sins shall obtain mercy.
>
> Proverbs 28:13

By His grace, God will save anyone who will receive Him.

> For it is by free grace (God's unmerited favor) that you are saved (delivered from judgment and made partakers of Christ's salvation) through [your] faith. And this [salvation] is not of yourselves — of your own doing, it came not through your own striving — but it is the gift of God;
>
> Not because of works [not the fulfillment of the Law's demands], lest any man should boast. — It is not the result of what any one can possibly do, so no one can pride himself in it or take glory to himself.
>
> Ephesians 2:8,9

Romans 10:9-11 says to believe in your heart and confess it with your mouth to step from a life of sin into the family of God. As you take this step, you will never be disappointed.

> Because if you acknowledge and confess with your lips that Jesus is Lord and in your heart believe (adhere to, trust in and rely on the truth) that God raised Him from the dead, you will be saved.

> For with the heart a person believes (adheres to, trusts in and relies on Christ) and so is justified (declared righteous, acceptable to God), and with the mouth he confesses — declares openly and speaks out freely his faith — and confirms [his] salvation.
>
> The Scripture says, No man who believes in Him — who adheres to, relies on and trusts in Him — will [ever] be put to shame or be disappointed.

If you once accepted Jesus Christ as your Lord and Savior but have been seduced into a perverted sexual life, *repent and confess your sin . . . then go and sin no more.*

> If we [freely] admit that we have sinned and confess our sins, He is faithful and just [true to His own nature and promises] and will forgive our sins (dismiss our lawlessness) and continuously cleanse us from all unrighteousness — everything not in conformity to His will in purpose, thought and action.

1 John 1:9

2. *Pray to be delivered and healed from actual perversion.*

> Confess to one another therefore your faults — your slips, your false steps, your offenses, your sins; and pray [also] for one another, that you may be healed and restored — to a spiritual tone of mind and heart. The earnest (heartfelt, continued) prayer of a righteous man makes tremendous power available — dynamic in its working.

James 5:16

3. *Be baptized with the Holy Spirit.*

> But you shall receive power — ability, efficiency and might — when the Holy Spirit has come upon you; and you shall be My witnesses in Jerusalem and all Judea and Samaria and to the ends — the very bounds — of the earth.

Acts 1:8

When you were born again, the Holy Spirit came to reside in you. When you ask Jesus to baptize you with the fire of the Holy Spirit, He will also come upon you, empowering you in a dimension you have never known. The power of the Holy Spirit which comes as a result of the baptism with the Spirit will strengthen you to resist Satan and his goods, whether it be sexual perversion or other sins.

4. *Take the yoke of Christ upon you.*

> Take My yoke upon you, and learn of Me; for I am gentle (meek) and humble (lowly) in heart, and you will find rest — relief, ease and refreshment and recreation and blessed quiet — for your souls.
>
> For My yoke is wholesome (useful, good) — not harsh, hard, sharp or pressing, but comfortable, gracious and pleasant; and My burden is light and easy to be borne.
>
> Matthew 11:29,30

5. *Read the Word of God daily.* (If you do not stay grounded in the Word, Satan will abort the blessings God has planned for you before you ever see them!)

> Every word of God is tried and purified; He is a shield to those who trust and take refuge in Him.
>
> Proverbs 30:5
>
> But He replied, It has been written, Man shall not live and be upheld and sustained by bread alone, but by every word that comes forth from the mouth of God.
>
> Matthew 4:4
>
> My son, attend to my words; consent and submit to my sayings.
>
> Let them not depart from your sight; keep them in the center of your heart.
>
> For they are life to those who find them, healing and health to all their flesh.
>
> Keep your heart with all vigilance and above all that you guard, for out of it flow the springs of life.
>
> Proverbs 4:20-23

6. *Learn to trust in the Lord.*

> Trust (lean on, rely on and be confident) in the Lord, and do good; so shall you dwell in the land and feed surely on His faithfulness, and truly you shall be fed.
>
> Psalm 37:3
>
> And whatever you ask for in prayer, having faith and [really] believing, you will receive.
>
> Matthew 21:22

> Truly, I tell you, whoever says to this mountain, Be lifted up and thrown into the sea! and does not doubt at all in his heart, but believes that what he says will take place, it will be done for him.

> For this reason I am telling you, whatever you ask for in prayer, believe — trust and be confident — that it is granted to you, and you will [get it].

> Mark 11:23,24

7. *Learn to fear the Lord*. To fear the Lord is to obey Him.

> In the reverent and worshipful fear of the Lord is strong confidence, and His children shall always have a place of refuge.

> Proverbs 14:26

> The reverent, worshipful fear of the Lord leads to life, and he who has it shall rest satisfied; he cannot be visited with [actual] evil

> Proverbs 19:23

> The reverent and worshipful fear of the Lord prolongs one's days, but the years of the wicked shall be made short.

> Proverbs 10:27

8. *Learn to abide in the Lord.*

> If you live in Me — abide vitally united to Me — and My words remain in you and continue to live in your hearts, ask whatever you will and it shall be done for you.

> John 15:7

9. *Put on the armor of God every day.*

Satan never quits in his subtle efforts to trip you up. Seducing spirits are on the move to get you to participate in perverse sexual sins. If every part of your armor is intact, you will not bow to Satan's tactics, whether it be sex sins or other sins.

> In conclusion, be strong in the Lord — be empowered through your union with Him; draw your strength from Him — that strength which His [boundless] might provides.

> Put on God's whole armor — the armor of a heavy-armed soldier, which God supplies — that you may be able

successfully to stand up against [all] the strategies and the deceits of the devil.

For we are not wrestling with flesh and blood — contending only with physical opponents — but against the despotisms, against the powers, against [the master spirits who are] the world rulers of this present darkness, against the spirit forces of wickedness in the heavenly (supernatural) sphere.

Therefore put on God's complete armor, that you may be able to resist and stand your ground on the evil day [of danger], and having done all [the crisis demands], to stand [firmly in your place].

Stand therefore — hold your ground — having tightened the belt of truth around your loins, and having put on the breastplate of integrity and of moral rectitude and right standing with God;

And having shod your feet in preparation [to face the enemy with the firm-footed stability, the promptness and the readiness produced by the good news] of the Gospel of peace.

Lift up over all the (covering) shield of saving faith, upon which you can quench all the flaming missiles of the wicked [one].

And take the helmet of salvation and the sword the Spirit wields, which is the Word of God.

Pray at all times — on every occasion, in every season — in the Spirit, with all [manner of] prayer and entreaty. To that end keep alert and watch with strong purpose and perseverance, interceding in behalf of all the saints (God's consecrated people).

Ephesians 6:10-18

10. *Pray without ceasing . . . pray with your understanding, and pray in the Spirit.*

. . . I will pray with my spirit — by the Holy Spirit that is within me; but I will also pray intelligently — with my mind and understanding; I will sing with my spirit — by the Holy Spirit that is within me; but I will sing (intelligently) with my mind and understanding also.

1 Corinthians 14:15

11. *Ask God daily for His wisdom.*

Show me Your ways, O Lord; teach me Your paths.

Guide me in Your truth and faithfulness and teach me,
for You are the God of my salvation.

Psalm 25:4,5a

Remember that you have the mind of Christ, and
nothing is impossible for those who are in Christ Jesus.

. . . But we have the mind of Christ, the Messiah, and
do hold the thoughts (feelings and purposes) of His heart.

1 Corinthians 2:16b

12. *Separate yourself from wrong relationships, for you will
truly become like those you hang around with.*

Do not be unequally yoked up with unbelievers — do
not make mismated alliances with them, or come under a
different yoke with them [inconsistent with your faith]. For
what partnership have right living and right standing with
God with iniquity and lawlessness? or how can light fellow-
ship with darkness?

What harmony can there be between Christ and Belial
[the devil]? Or what has a believer in common with an
unbeliever?

What agreement [can there be between] a temple of God
and idols? For we are the temple of the living God; even as
God said, I will dwell in and with and among them and will
walk in and with and among them, and I will be their God,
and they shall be My people.

So, come out from among (unbelievers), and separate
(sever) yourselves from them, says the Lord, and touch not
[any] unclean thing; then I will receive you kindly and treat
you with favor,

And I will be a Father to you, and you shall be My sons
and daughters, says the Lord Almighty.

2 Corinthians 6:14-18

As you submit yourself totally to God and daily seek
Him first, new direction will come to you . . . new and
exciting doors will open unto you.

Remember, the best is yet to come when you yield to
the Master. He will talk with you and walk with you now

that you have made the decision to leave the old flesh-dominated life behind.

13. *Make a decision to walk in love.* You will have plenty of opportunities to get into strife, but resist them in the same manner that you would resist a deadly plague. Meditate daily upon 1 Corinthians 13:4-8:

> Love endures long and is patient and kind; love never is envious nor boils over with jealousy; it is not boastful or vainglorious, does not display itself haughtily.
>
> It is not conceited — arrogant and inflated with pride; it is not rude (unmannerly), and does not act unbecomingly. Love [God's love in us] does not insist on its own rights or its own way, for it is not self-seeking; it is not touchy or fretful or resentful; it takes no account of the evil done to it — pays no attention to a suffered wrong.
>
> It does not rejoice at injustice and unrighteousness, but rejoices when right and truth prevail.
>
> Love bears up under anything and everything that comes, is ever ready to believe the best of every person, its hopes are fadeless under all circumstances and it endures everything [without weakening].
>
> Love never fails — never fades out or becomes obsolete or comes to an end . . . .

14. Develop an unshakable confidence in God and His promises, for your confidence will bring great reward.

> For we have become fellows with Christ, the Messiah, and share in all He has for us, if only we hold our first newborn confidence and original assured expectation [in virtue of which we are believers] firm and unshaken to the end.
>
> Hebrews 3:14
>
> Do not, therefore, fling away your fearless confidence, for it carries a great and glorious compensation of reward.
>
> For you have need of steadfast patience and endurance, so that you may perform and fully accomplish the will of God, and thus receive and carry away [and enjoy to the full] what is promised.
>
> Hebrews 10:35,36

Suggestions for Staying
Under God's Blessing Spout

Here are a few simple and practical suggestions that will help establish you in your new life in Christ.

1. *Memorize Scripture promises on who you are in Christ.* This will strengthen your self-image (Christ's image in you) . . . it will help you to know that you are a beautiful person . . . that God has no record of your past . . . and if you have not done so already, it will help you to forgive yourself.

I would recommend that you meditate on all of the Scripture presented in Kenneth E. Hagin's minibook, *In Him.*[12]

2. *Memorize at least three (3) additional Scripture verses each day. Satan cannot move you when you are grounded in God's Word.*

3. *Never leave home without putting on the whole armor of God.* (Eph. 6:10-18.)

4. *Stay away from the old crowd* . . . make new friends . . . friends who will uplift, strengthen, and encourage you in the Lord.

5. *Find a solid, Word-based church home, and get involved* in some area of the ministry where you can give out the life of Christ in you to others.

6. *Set new goals.*

7. *Through prayer and a daily intake of God's Word, allow the fruit of the Holy Spirit to mature in your own human spirit* — love, joy, patience, kindness, goodness, faithfulness, meekness, gentleness, and self-control.

8. *You may enjoy taking a Bible Class from a solid, Word-based Bible School in your community.* (Remember, also, that many ministries today offer correspondence Bible School programs through which you can complete your studies within your own home.[13])

9. *Pursue a worthwhile, constructive hobby.*

10. *Claim a new gift from God.* (For example, the gift of writing, speaking, or playing an instrument.)

11. *Develop your good qualities, and prune your bad qualities through the Word and prayer.* (Intimate time with God will develop His nature and characteristics within you.)

12. *Never gossip about the old life.* Let it remain dead, for the "old you" no longer exists. Build your new life around who and what God says you are!

You are well on your way to clothing yourself with God's garments of holiness and to living and walking in the God-kind of love. Hallelujah!

> . . . Holiness [apparent in separation from sin, with simple trust and hearty obedience] is becoming to Your house, O Lord, for ever.

Psalm 93:5

---

[12] Available from:
Kenneth Hagin Ministries
P. O. Box 50126
Tulsa, OK 74150-0126.

[13] Also available from RHEMA Bible Training Center, or Kenneth Hagin Ministries, at above address.

CONCLUSION

A perverted sex life is like heading to Hell on a banana peel . . . it is the fastest way to Hell and destruction that I am aware of. A person involved in perverted sex is dead while he (or she) yet lives.

Get up today and walk away completely from your old life. You cannot do it in yourself, but in Christ, you can. As you take this step, you will soon be able to say: *Father, because of Jesus Christ and His shed blood, my new life in You is the highest and best life I have ever tasted.*

Once you have tasted pure, genuine love, you will never desire the counterfeit — homosexuality, lesbianism, love of money, praise of men, or lust in any other form.

Let us examine the words of Jesus spoken through John as recorded in Revelation. I believe it will encourage you to move on into holiness now.

He who is unrighteous (unjust, wicked) let him be unrighteous still, and he that is filthy (vile, impure) let him be filthy still, and he that is righteous (just, upright, in right standing with God) let him do right still, and he who is holy let him be holy still.

Behold, I (Jesus) am coming soon, and I shall bring My wages and rewards with Me, to repay and render to each one just what his own actions and his own work merit.

I am the Alpha and the Omega, the First and the Last (the Before all and at the End of all).

Blessed (happy and to be envied) are those who cleanse their garments that they may have the authority and right to [approach] the tree of life and to enter in through the gates to the city.

[But] without are the dogs and those who practice sorceries (magic arts) and impurity (the lewd, adulterers) and the murderers and idolaters and every one who loves and deals in falsehood — untruth, error, deception, cheating.

I, Jesus, have sent My messenger (angel) to you to witness and to give you assurance of these things for the churches (assemblies). I am [both] the Root (the Source) and the Offspring of David, the radiant and brilliant Morning Star.

The (Holy) Spirit and the bride [the church, the true Christians] say, Come! And let him who is listening say, Come! And let every one come who is thirsty [who is painfully conscious of his need of those things by which the soul is refreshed, supported and strengthened]; and whoever [earnestly] desires to do it, let him come and take and appropriate (drink) the Water of Life without cost . . . .

[Surely] I am coming quickly — swiftly, speedily. Amen — so let it be! Yes, come, Lord Jesus!

The grace (blessing and favor) of the Lord Jesus Christ, the Messiah be with all the saints — God's holy people [those set apart for God, to be, as it were, exclusively His]. Amen — so let it be!

Revelation 22:11-17, 20b,21

If this book is not available at your local bookstore,
you may purchase additional copies from:

Albury Press
P. O. Box 55388
Tulsa, Oklahoma 74155-1388

1-800-826-5992
918-584-5535

For ministry inquiries, please write:

Barbara Hicks Seguin
Author of Life Ministries, Inc.
P. O. Box 701860
Tulsa, Oklahoma 74170-1860

or

P. O. Box 3137
Center Line, Michigan 48015

NOTES

NOTES

NOTES

NOTES

NOTES

NOTES